AGS

Preparing for Writing Tests

Student Activity Book

GRADES 4–5

AGS®

AGS® American Guidance Service, Inc.
4201 Woodland Road
Circle Pines, MN 55014-1796
1-800-328-2560

Printed in the United States of America

ISBN 0-7854-2469-5

Product Number: 71502

A 0 9 8 7 6 5 4 3 2 1

Contents

Contents

INTRODUCTION

About Writing Tests

What Kinds of Questions Are Asked on Tests?

Tests have many kinds of questions. Here are some types of questions you might see:

- **Multiple Choice** You will often see these questions on tests. They ask you to pick out the best answer from a group of choices. You will see multiple-choice questions on many different tests. They can be found on reading, mathematics, science, and social studies tests.

- **Short Answer** or **Short Response** These questions ask you to write a few sentences to answer a question. The question is usually about something you have just read.

- **Essay Prompts** or **Extended Response** These questions are on writing tests. A prompt is a question. It asks you to write a long answer called an **essay.** Because you must write an essay, writing tests are sometimes called essay tests.

This book will focus on writing tests.

What Is the Purpose of a Writing Test?

First, let's see what a writing test does **not** do.

- A writing test does **not** test you on facts you have learned in class. The prompt will give you most of the information you need. Any other information will come from your own life.

- A writing test does **not** measure how neatly you write. The most important thing is that you have good ideas. Still, your handwriting must be clear enough to read. If it is not, no one will understand your ideas.

- A writing test does **not** measure how well you agree with your teacher (or anyone else). Many writing prompts ask you to take a side. In those cases, there is no "right" side to choose.

The purpose of a writing test is to measure two things. First, a writing test measures how well you can put ideas together. It also measures how clearly you can present them. In a writing test, you will have a limited amount of time to write your essay. Also, you will not be allowed to look in a dictionary or any other book. You cannot even ask a friend to look at your essay. A writing test measures your skill as a writer. It measures how well you write without books, teachers, or others to help you.

How Are Writing Tests Graded?

Answers on writing tests are graded by trained graders. These graders are sometimes called **readers.** Test readers are trained to be fair. When they are grading, they usually use a **rubric.** A rubric is a checklist. It lists the things a reader will look for in your essay. There are many kinds of rubrics. However, most rubrics center on the same things.

Rubrics often tell readers what to look for in an essay. They will ask for the following parts:

- a clear central idea, or **focus**
- information that backs up the central idea
- good order
- a clear beginning and end
- a complete answer to the prompt
- correct use of grammar, punctuation, and spelling

How Will This Book Help You on Writing Tests?

Writing tests can seem scary, but only if you are not ready for them. Luckily, this book will help you get ready. You will learn how to write the best essays you can. You will:

- learn what goes into different kinds of essays
- learn how to read essay prompts just like the ones you will see on tests
- learn and practice ways to plan an essay
- learn how to look at your essay like a trained reader
- learn how to find and fix your writing mistakes

Finally, you will get lots of practice. This will make you an experienced writer. You will be ready for any writing test.

WRITING FOR AN ESSAY TEST

Introduction

On a writing test, you may have to write an essay or paragraph to answer a question. An essay is a group of paragraphs that work together for a purpose. To write an essay for a test, you must first read the question carefully. Then, think about how you will answer. You want to write the best answer that you can. That means coming up with a clear focus, strong information, and a good order.

Focus

An essay should be about just one idea. We will call this idea the **focus** or **central idea.** You should write your focus in just one sentence. This sentence might be a point your writing will prove. It might also tell the reader what you will say in your essay. Think of the focus as a guide for the rest of your answer on the writing test.

Example Focus:

> **"Our town should work to clean up the beach."**

Support

Most of your essay will be made up of sentences that support your focus. These sentences can include the following:

- ideas
- proof
- reasons
- explanations
- examples
- details

All of these together are called the **support.** You can use as many kinds of support as you need in a single answer. Your support should always be about your focus.

Example Supporting Reason:

> **"Not many people use the beach because it is full of weeds."**

Order

Clear order helps your readers know what you are saying. Imagine that you are writing an answer to a test question. If your information is not in a clear order, you will confuse your reader.

When you answer a writing question, think about what order you want to put your information in. You should have an opening thought, a body, and a closing thought.

Your opening thought tells the reader about your focus for the first time. The body of your writing is made up of support for your focus. Your closing thought states your focus again. The closing thought will also sum up the main points you made in the support section.

In longer essays, the opening and closing thoughts will each take a paragraph. Each supporting point might have its own paragraph. For some writing questions, your answer may be only a few sentences long. Still, your answer should have an opening thought, a body, and a closing thought.

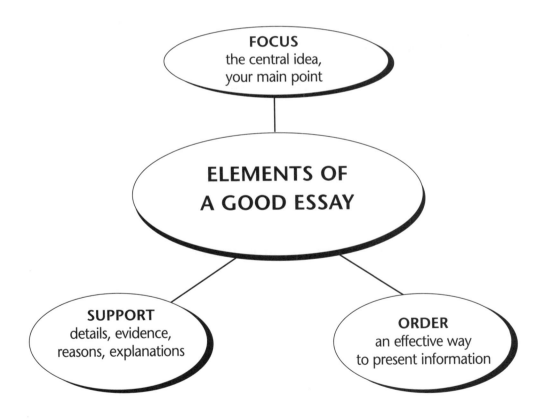

To do well on a writing test, you must find and support your focus. You also need to order your information clearly. With practice, you will be able to write a clear focus. You will be able to back up your focus with strong support. Last, you will learn how to choose the best order for your writing. Then, you will be well on your way to doing well on essay tests.

Focusing Your Essay

When you write, your essay must have a clear focus. The focus is the central idea of your writing. Every part of your writing will have to do with the focus. Here are some things to keep in mind when you think of your focus:

- Your focus must respond to the question.
- Your focus must not be too narrow or too wide.
- Limit your focus to one sentence.
- Put your focus near the end of your first paragraph.
- Once you pick a focus, make sure that everything you write is related to it.

Getting Started

The question you answer in a writing test is called a **prompt.** Read the following prompt. Then, read the focus sentences below it. Choose the focus that best answers the question. Be ready to explain your choice.

> **Prompt** Imagine your class is planning to do some volunteer work. What kind of project do you want your class to choose, and why?

Sample Focuses

1. Our class should plant trees in the park.

2. We need to do volunteer work, so we should have a canned-food drive.

3. Our class should work at the local library because we all use the books and the librarians need some good helpers.

4. The relief kitchen is a good place for volunteers.

5. The Clean-the-Community litter control program would be a good idea for our class volunteer project.

Looking It Over

Now, rewrite the sentences that you did not choose. Make them into good focus sentences. Remember that they must be about a kind of volunteer work. They should also tell why your class should select that work.

1. _____

_____

2. _____

_____

3. _____

_____

4. _____

_____

Trying It Out

Choose one of the following prompts. Write a focus sentence that answers it.

Prompt A What was your favorite year or grade in school? Write a short essay about your favorite year. Explain why it was special to you.

Prompt B Some people learn more when they work in groups in school. Others feel they learn more when they work alone. Write an essay telling how you like to work. Explain why you feel you learn more when you work this way.

Your Focus:

_____

_____

_____

Supporting the Central Idea

You need more than a good central idea in order to do well on a writing test. First, you should state your focus in the opening. Then, you must tell more about it in the body of your writing. Each body paragraph should begin with a topic sentence. The topic sentence will introduce the support that follows it. This support can take many forms. The forms of support you choose will depend on the type of essay you are writing. You will want to choose from the following kinds of support in your writing tests:

- ideas
- examples
- reasons
- proof
- details
- explanations

Remember that a good essay needs to have a clear focus and strong support. Make sure that you can support your focus.

Getting Started

Read the prompt and focus below. Then, read the topic sentences that follow. They are topic sentences for the body paragraphs of the essay. Circle the number in front of each sentence that supports the focus.

Prompt Think about your favorite subject in school. Write a short essay telling why this is your favorite subject.

Sample Focus

Art is my favorite subject because it makes me think and see in new ways.

Sample Topic Sentences

1. I really like drawing because it is the easiest kind of art.
2. When I sculpt, I look at things in new ways.
3. I learned how to see things as if I were seeing them for the first time.
4. I like to paint pictures of flowers, trees, and people.
5. I found that there are more colors in the world than I knew.
6. Paintings are good to hang on walls.
7. I have learned a lot from the way other artists look at the world.
8. Clay can be tough to work with because it dries quickly.

Looking It Over

Now, choose three of the sentences you selected from the last activity. Use them to fill in the following graphic organizer.

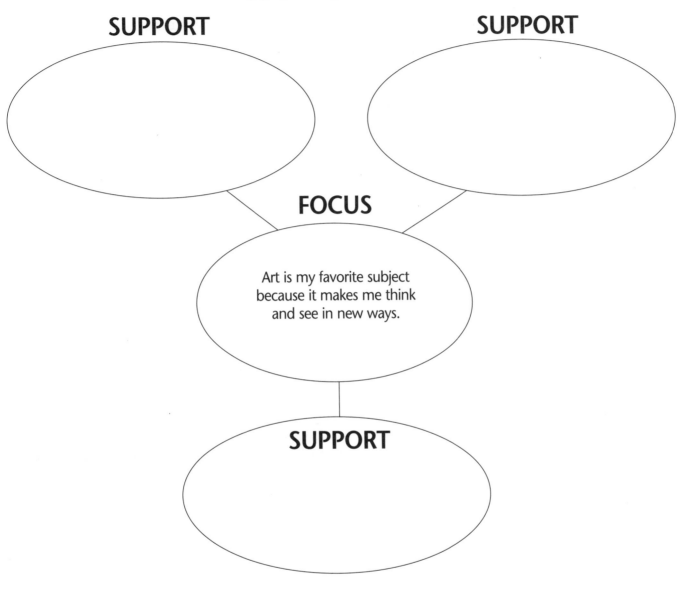

SUPPORT

SUPPORT

FOCUS

Art is my favorite subject because it makes me think and see in new ways.

SUPPORT

Trying It Out

Read the following prompt. Then, write a focus and three supporting sentences. Use your own paper.

Prompt Some schools in your town are open year-round. They have several short breaks instead of a long summer vacation. Other schools in your town are open for nine months. They have one long vacation during the summer. Decide which you think is better. Write a focus and three supporting topic sentences. Explain why you feel the way you do.

Ordering Your Essay

First, you must narrow your essay's focus. Next, you need to collect support for that focus. Then, you are ready to think about **ordering.** Ordering means the way an essay's ideas are put together. An essay usually has three parts:

- The **opening thought** is a paragraph that catches the reader's interest. It includes the focus of the essay.

- The **body** is one or more paragraphs. The body contains ideas that support the focus.

- The **closing thought** is a paragraph that states the focus again. It sums up the main points.

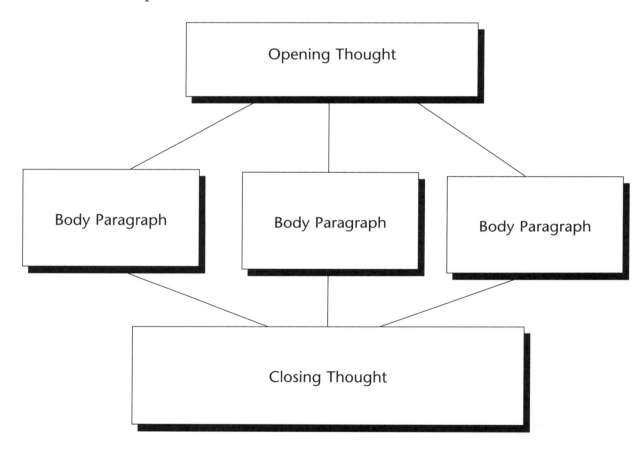

Getting Started

Read the prompt below and the sample essay on the next page. Look for ways to improve the way the essay is ordered.

Prompt Think about all the teachers you have had since you started school. Who were your favorite teachers? Choose one and write a paper that tells why your favorite teacher was so special.

A Living Example
by Nida Asara

A | Mrs. Milne always made class fun. She made up rhymes to help us learn math. She helped us write plays. We acted them out in groups. Even art was more fun with her. She helped us use our imaginations. She wanted us to come up with our own ideas. With her help, we did. | 1 2 3 4 5

B | A truly good teacher can really help students. Mrs. Milne was my third-grade teacher. I don't think I will ever have a better teacher. Mrs. Milne knew how to make learning fun. She also knew how to help students when learning was hard. She truly cared about her students. | 6 7 8 9 10

C | Mrs. Milne also helped when her students had trouble. Mrs. Milne stayed after school to help me read. She spent many hours teaching me how to sound out long words. Sometimes, I felt bad about myself. Even then, she could still see my strengths. I thought I would never read well. She helped me see that I could learn. | 11 12 13 14 15

D | Mrs. Milne taught that I can learn anything if I put my mind to it. Sometimes I have to work harder than other kids. Still, I know I will do well if I keep trying. I often think of the two sayings she put up in the classroom: "Never give up on anything, especially not on yourself," and "Believe in amazing things—believe in yourself." | 16 17 18 19 20

E | All of Mrs. Milne's students can remember how much she cared about us. She stayed after school to help teach me. She did the same for many of my friends, too. When we were upset, she reminded us that everyone had trouble sometimes. She taught us that it was all right to feel sad as long as we did not quit trying. | 21 22 23 24 25

Looking It Over

On your paper, answer these questions.

1. Which paragraph states the essay's focus? Write the focus in your own words.

2. In paragraph A, Nida tells about things her teacher did with the class. How does this support the focus?

3. List three points or ideas from the essay that support the idea that Nida's teacher was a great teacher.

4. How do the sentences in paragraph D sum up the essay's main points?

5. Write the paragraph letters in the correct order. The opening thought should be first. The closing thought should be last.

Writing on Your Own

Now, you have learned about what makes an essay good. It is time to practice what you have learned. In this lesson, you will write an essay. You will need your own paper.

Getting Started

1. **Reading the Prompt:** Before you write an essay for a test, read the prompt carefully.

- Read the whole prompt twice.

- Underline key words, such as **describe, explain, compare, tell,** or **persuade.**

Now, use these two steps with this prompt:

> **Prompt** Some parents teach their children at home. These children do not go to a school. They still learn using textbooks, tests, and papers just like school. Parents home-school their children for many reasons. Think about the good points and bad points of teaching children at home. How do you feel about home-schooling and why?

2. **Brainstorming:** Now, you have read the prompt twice. You have underlined some of the important parts of the prompt. You are ready to move on to the next step: brainstorming. Try to come up with as many ideas as you can. For this essay, you will order your ideas. Use the titles **good points** and **bad points.** Use this chart to write your ideas down. Use your own paper if you need more space.

Good Points	Bad Points
might get to spend more time on lessons that are hard (student will not be rushed)	might not learn everything they should

Now, go through your list. Think about each item. Select either three good points or three bad points. Make sure you will be able to support them well. A strong essay will have a clear focus and good support. You should only choose ideas that you can write about.

3. Writing the Focus: First, finish choosing the best ideas from your list of good points and bad points. Then, you can write your focus.

Keep these things in mind when you work on your focus:

- The focus should answer the question that the prompt asks.

- The focus should be one sentence.

Think about what you want to say about home-schooling. Did you find more good points than bad points, or the other way around? You could decide that it is a good idea to home-school a student. Then, your focus might sound like this:

Sample Focus

Students who are home-schooled are lucky because their lessons and their "school" are both set up just for them.

Now, write your own focus sentence. Use your own paper.

4. Supporting the Focus: After you write your focus, you can make an outline. Fill the outline with your supporting ideas.

Sample Outline

Focus: Students who are home-schooled are lucky because their lessons and their "school" are both set up just for them.

I. learn at their own pace
   A. spend more time figuring out lessons that are hard
   B. might not have to spend much time on easy lessons
II. more time and attention on lessons
   A. probably not as worried about having the latest clothes or games
   B. don't have to worry about being teased or bothered by other kids
III. good teaching
   A. parents know their children and what will be easy or hard for them
   B. teacher (parent) puts all his or her energy into one or two students

Now use a separate sheet of paper to make your own outline.

5. Writing a First Draft: Use your outline to help you write a **draft** of your essay. When you write an essay, your first try is called a draft. A draft usually has errors you need to correct. Use a separate sheet of paper to write your first draft.

- Write the body paragraphs first.

- Then, go back and write your opening thought and closing thought.

- State your focus in the opening thought. State it again in the closing thought.

- Make sure you put the paragraphs in an order that makes sense.

- Read over your draft. Check for correct spelling and punctuation.

Grading an Essay

It is good to know how your writing will be graded. That way, you can raise your score on a test. You will know what the graders want to see. Then, you can work to make your writing better.

Your test will be graded by someone who is trained to judge writing. This grader will use a **rubric** to score your paper. The rubric will help the grader check the essay. It will remind the grader to check for focus, support, and order. The rubric will also remind the grader to check for clearness, spelling, and punctuation. In this lesson, you will practice using rubrics to score writing. Then, you will use a rubric to score the paper that you wrote in Lesson 4.

Getting Started

Read the prompt and the two opening thoughts.

Prompt People have probably asked you what you want to be when you grow up. Think of some of the jobs that you might like. Choose one that you know about. Write a paper telling why you might want to hold that job when you are an adult.

Sample Opening Thought A

When I grow up, I want to be a firefighter. I do not know of any job that is more exciting than that. I would get to fight fires and help people. I might even save a life. Another reason to be a firefighter would be to help my town. I am also very strong. That would help me as a firefighter or as a police officer. I would like to be a police officer, too. I think riding on the firetruck would be more fun than riding in a police car.

Sample Opening Thought B

There are many jobs to choose from. It can be hard to decide. If I had to decide now, I think I would want to be a doctor. Doctors have to like science, and I do. Doctors have to enjoy helping people, too. I think helping people is the best thing you can do. Doctors also need to go to school for a long time. Luckily, I like school. All of these things make me think I might like to be a doctor.

Looking It Over

Use the rubric below to grade the two opening thoughts. Rate each item on a scale from one to five. Five is the best rating.

Rubric	Score (A)	Score (B)
The opening thought catches the reader's attention.		
The opening thought leads into the topic.		
The opening thought states the focus.		
The focus is clear. It is not too narrow or too broad.		

Trying It Out

Now, you have practiced using rubrics. You know how to grade writing. Use a rubric to grade the paper you wrote for Lesson 4 on page 17.

Rubric	Score (1–5)
The opening thought catches the reader's attention.	
The opening thought leads into the topic. It states the focus of the paper.	
The focus is clear. It is not too narrow or too broad.	
Each body paragraph has a clear main idea. The main idea supports the focus.	
Each body paragraph supports its own main idea.	
The body paragraphs are in an order that makes sense.	
The closing thought states the focus again.	
The paper follows rules for spelling and writing clear sentences.	

CHAPTER 1 REVIEW

In this chapter, you have learned what goes into a good essay. You have learned what a focus is. You have learned about how to support a focus. Last, you have learned how to put your paragraphs in an order that makes sense. Knowing these things will help you get high scores on writing tests.

Looking Back

Answer the following questions on the lines provided.

1. What is a focus? How long should a focus be?

   _____

2. Where should the focus be found in an essay? Where should the focus be stated again?

   _____

3. What sorts of things make up support?

   _____

4. Where should support be found in an essay?

   _____

5. What is a prompt?

   _____

6. Why should you put your paragraphs in a good order?

   _____

   _____

Trying It Out

Now, you will use what you have learned. You will write an essay on your own. Read the prompt below. Then, write your essay on a separate piece of paper. When you are done, use the rubric on page 19 to score your writing.

> **Prompt** Imagine that your school is getting a new name. The school will be named after someone who is NOT famous. The person could be a student, a teacher, or someone else living in your area. The person should be important to the school in some way. Write an essay telling whom you think the school should be named after and why.

STEPS IN PLANNING YOUR ESSAY

Introduction

To do well on a writing test, you must plan your essay before you start writing. The steps for planning are as follows:

- reading the prompt
- gathering your thoughts
- highlighting the central idea
- ordering your support ideas

Here is a short explanation of the steps.

Reading the Prompt

Read the prompt carefully to find out what to write in your answer. For example, the prompt might tell you to write about how two things are different.

Gathering Your Thoughts

To gather your thoughts, write down what you might include in your answer. You might write down facts, examples, and reasons. While planning, you may write these things down in any order.

Highlighting the Central Idea

In this step, you will choose one central idea. You will build your answer around this idea. It will be the focus of your answer.

Ordering Your Support Ideas

The last planning step is to order the ideas that support your focus. You will decide where to place each of the support ideas in your essay.

You will learn more about each of these steps in the lessons of this chapter. When you have planned your answer step by step, you will be able to write a good answer. You will also be able to tell how well you have answered the prompt.

Reading the Prompt

The first step in planning a good essay is to read the prompt carefully. Read it slowly. Read it at least two times.

As you read the prompt, try to answer these questions:

- What **topic,** or subject, does the prompt ask me to write about? (The prompt below asks you to write about **your favorite hobby.** This is the topic.)

- Who will read my essay? (The prompt below says to write for a **classmate.** The classmate is your **audience.** If the prompt does not name an audience, you should write to a **general audience.** A general audience is anyone who might be interested in the topic of your essay.)

- What **kind of information** does the prompt ask for? (The prompt asks for the **name of the hobby.** The prompt also asks **why it is your favorite.** This information is sometimes called the **purpose.**)

Prompt What is your favorite hobby? Give a classmate two reasons why this activity is your favorite.

Getting Started

Read these prompts carefully. Then, answer the questions.

Prompt A Briefly write a story about an animal.

Prompt B Name your favorite exercise. Give a friend two reasons why it is your favorite.

Prompt C Describe a time when you were disappointed. Explain why you were disappointed. Imagine that you are telling someone you do not know.

Prompt D If you could have any job you want when you grow up, what would it be? Explain why.

Looking It Over

Answer the questions about the prompts in **Getting Started** on page 22.

1. What is the topic of prompt A?

   _____

2. What kind of information does prompt A ask for?

   _____

3. How many things will you need to do for prompt A?

   _____

4. What is the topic of prompt B?

   _____

5. What kind of information does prompt B ask for?

   _____

6. How many things will you need to do for prompt B?

   _____

7. What is the topic of prompt C?

   _____

8. What kind of information does prompt C ask for?

   _____

9. How many things will you need to do for prompt C?

   _____

10. What is the topic of prompt D?

   _____

11. What kind of information does prompt D ask for?

   _____

12. How many things will you need to do for prompt D?

   _____

Gathering Your Thoughts

Once you understand the prompt, you can start gathering your thoughts. You know you need to come up with a **topic.** You can begin to find topic ideas by **prewriting.** When you prewrite, set a time limit for yourself. Then, come up with as many ideas as you can in that time.

- **Brainstorming** or **freewriting**—First, you write down the topic of the prompt. Then, write down any topic idea that comes into your mind. Your ideas do not have to make sense. You do not have to write complete sentences. Punctuation does not need to be perfect either. You are only writing to come up with ideas.

- Making a **cluster diagram**—Write all your thoughts in clusters of circles. If your topic was "chores," you would write this topic in a circle in the middle of your paper. Around that circle, you would draw other circles for each of your ideas and connect them to the center circle with lines.

Getting Started

Read the prompt below. Study the sample freewriting list and cluster diagram carefully. Remember that the writer will choose one focus idea for his or her essay.

Prompt Name a chore that you do to help around the house. Tell what it is like and how you do it.

Maryam Cheney's Freewriting
Topic: Chores

chores, hmm, let's see, there's taking out the trash, clearing the table, washing dishes, folding laundry, what else? oh yeah, cleaning my room. ugh that's the worst, but it sure is nice to have my room clean afterwards. Mom always says that a clean room is the reward I get for cleaning. My system: dishes first, then trash, clothes, and anything else. it takes a lot longer than clearing the table or taking out the trash. Sometimes the trash stinks-no fun. And then there's getting up early on Wednesday mornings to take the big trash cans to the corner for the garbage collectors. Don't have much to say about trash though. Hmm. I just don't know what to write about.

Maryam Cheney's Cluster Diagram

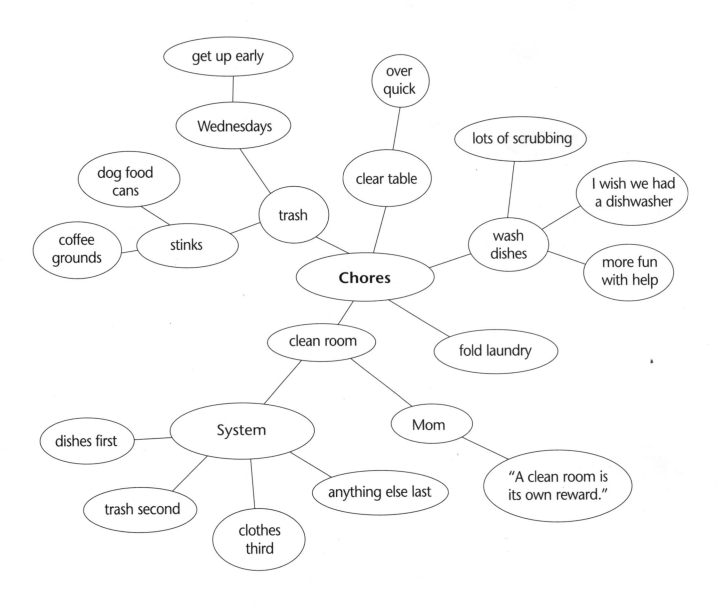

Looking It Over

Now, look at Maryam's freewriting and cluster diagram samples. Answer these questions.

1. Which topic do you think Maryam should choose? Why?

    _____

    _____

2. Choose two topics that Maryam should cut. Why should Maryam cut these topics?

    _____

    _____

3. How could the cluster diagram be more helpful than freewriting?

    _____

    _____

4. How could freewriting be more helpful than the cluster diagram?

    _____

    _____

Trying It Out

Now try prewriting on your own. You can freewrite or make a cluster diagram. Come up with topic ideas for the following prompt. Do not forget to set a time limit of five minutes. Write on your own paper.

Prompt To decorate the classroom, your teacher wants to have a picture of each student. These could be photographs, pictures drawn by the students, or pictures drawn by someone who is not in the class. In the pictures, students will be doing things they enjoy. What would your picture be like?

Highlighting the Central Idea

You have already learned to get ideas by prewriting. Now you will learn how to build your essay around your best idea.

This idea will be your **central idea** or **focus.** A focus is a sentence that gives a direct answer to the prompt. The focus is often near the end of the opening thought of the essay. It contains the main idea that the rest of the essay will talk about. Remember, everything you write should relate to the focus.

Look at the following prompt and focus sentences:

Prompt Your school staff recently put up posters that are supposed to get students to read more books. The posters show famous young stars reading. Each poster has a quote from the actor. All the quotes are about how reading is "cool." Do you think posters like this work? Explain why or why not in an essay.

Sample Focus A

Our school's new reading posters will work because students want to be like stars.

Sample Focus B

Schools should not use these posters because they do not work.

Focus A is a strong answer to the prompt for these reasons:

- It clearly states the focus of the essay.
- It responds to all parts of the prompt.
- It is not too narrow or too broad.
- It is only one sentence long.

Focus B is weaker for these reasons:

- The explanation "because they do not work" is too broad.
- The focus is unclear. The focus does not tell why the posters do not work.

Getting Started

Now, try looking at some focus sentences for yourself. Read the prompt. Then, read the focus sentences carefully. Remember what makes a focus sentence good.

Prompt Imagine that your school is going to build a new playground. Name the one thing you most want to see built on the new playground. Explain your choice.

Sample Focus Sentences

A. The new playground should have a merry-go-round because many students can use it at once.

B. I think the new playground should have a roller coaster.

C. A new playground would be a waste of money. We should have better cafeteria food instead.

D. It is important for students to have really fun stuff on the playground.

E. The best thing we could build on the new playground would be a jungle gym because students need exercise.

Looking It Over

Answer these questions about the sample focus sentences.

1. Which sample focuses do you think are the strongest? Why?

   _____

2. Which sample focuses do not answer the question the prompt asks?

   _____

3. Is focus B a strong answer to the prompt? Explain your answer.

   _____

4. Rewrite focus D. Add the missing parts that would make it a strong focus.

   _____

5. What is wrong with focus C?

   _____

6. Write your own focus to respond to the prompt.

   _____

Trying It Out

Read the prompts below. Choose one to work with. Use the space below or your own paper to brainstorm. Then, write a focus for one of the prompts.

Prompt A Some children ride the bus to school. Other children live close enough to walk. Which do you think would be better? Give your reasons in an essay.

Prompt B Many parents are worried that their children will be harmed by playing video games. They worry that children are not spending enough time reading or playing outside. Do you think that video games are harmful? Write an essay that explains your answer.

Prompt C If you could no longer speak, how would you communicate with your friends? Explain your answer.

Your Focus:

_____

_____

_____

_____

Ordering Your Support Ideas

As you prewrite, you may see that some of your ideas fit together. Some of them may not fit at all. Ordering your ideas means putting them into an order that makes sense. The order of your ideas depends on what type of essay you are writing. Different kinds of essays need different ways of ordering. There are four main types of order.

- **Time order** is used to tell stories. This order can also be used to explain how to do something. A set of directions will begin with the first thing you should do.

- **Order of importance** is used to give reasons or details. Ideas may go from least important to most important. They can also go from most important to least important. Most lists of reasons are written in order of importance.

- **Order of place** is used to describe. Writers use this order when they want to tell where things are. For example, they may describe a room from left to right or front to back. They may even describe a scene from near to far.

- **Logical order** is used to define or explain. It is also used to show how things are alike or different. Writers use this order when they want to group related ideas together. For example, they may tell about cars in one part of an essay, and about planes in a different part.

Getting Started

Now, how do you decide which type of order is the best for your essay? Begin by sorting your ideas. There are many ways to do this. Two good ways are making a chart and using a diagram.

When you make a chart, you begin to order your prewriting notes. You decide which ideas or details belong together. Write your focus at the top of the chart. Then write **support ideas** at the top of each column. When you write your essay, you will explain each support idea in a paragraph of its own. These paragraphs will need **support details.** Those are details that support the paragraph's topic. On your chart, write the support details in the columns.

Look at the prompt and chart on the next page.

Many students in your school want to hold a canned food drive. They want to help feed the hungry. Write an essay to convince your school principal to sponsor a drive.

Satish's Chart

Focus: Our school should have a canned food drive because students who are involved would have many important experiences.		
Learn new skills	Have fun	Help other people
learn from people who help the hungry learn how to plan a big event	make posters run games	learn ways to help other people learn more about people who are in need

You can also use a diagram to sort your ideas. Most diagrams use circles or squares to show how ideas are connected. Look at the the following prompt and diagram.

Prompt Think of something that you know how to make. For example, you might know how to make a great toy, tool, or sandwich. Write an essay that tells someone else how to make that thing.

Orquidea's Diagram

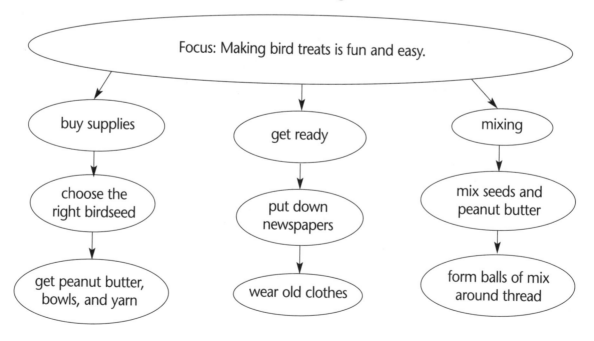

Looking It Over

1. How are Satish's chart and Orquidea's diagram the same?

   _____

   _____

2. How are the chart and the diagram different?

   _____

   _____

3. How do charts and diagrams help writers put ideas in order?

   _____

   _____

4. Imagine that Satish wants to put his chart into order of importance. He wants to go from most to least important. How should he order his paragraph topics?

   _____

   _____

5. What order does Orquidea use for the information in her diagram?

   _____

   _____

Trying It Out

Choose **one** of the following prompts. Arrange your ideas in a chart or diagram on your own paper.

Prompt A Write an essay that tells about the most useful thing you have ever learned. Think about why it is useful. Tell what made it useful to you.

Prompt B If you could create a holiday for anything, what would it be? Write an essay describing your new holiday and why people should celebrate it.

Writing on Your Own

More than once, you will take a test that asks you to write an essay. Where do you start? The prompt is usually the best place to begin.

In Lesson 1, you learned how to read a prompt. You already know that you can use a prompt to identify the topic, audience, and purpose of your essay.

- Topic—what the prompt asks you to write about
- Audience—whom the prompt asks you to write for
- Purpose—what the prompt asks you to do

Read the prompts below. Follow the steps to write an essay that responds to one of them.

Prompt A (Informative) Many times, students feel that schools do not do enough to stop teasing. What do you think about this? Write an essay showing that your school does or does not do enough to help students who are teased by other students.

Prompt B (Narrative) Write a story for your principal about a time when you or someone you know was teased. Your story should make a point about students who tease others.

Step 1. Decide which prompt to use. Then, on your own paper, write down the topic, audience, and purpose of an essay which responds to the prompt you chose.

Step 2. Use one of the prewriting methods you learned in Lesson 2 to gather ideas for your essay.

Step 3. Look at your prewriting and find a focus for your essay. Review Lesson 3 if you need to.

Step 4. Use one of the ordering methods you learned in Lesson 4 to decide on an order for your essay's paragraphs.

(continued on next page)

Step 5. Write your essay on the lines below.

_____

_____

_____

_____

_____

_____

_____

_____

_____

_____

_____

_____

_____

_____

_____

_____

_____

_____

_____

_____

_____

_____

Evaluating Your Writing

Evaluate is a word that means "judge." Evaluating your writing means judging it. As you do, you can make it better. People who score tests will go over your writing closely. In this lesson, you will learn to see what graders see. Then, you will look for the same things in your own writing. That way, you can improve your scores on writing tests.

Getting Started

The person who scores your essay will look for certain things:

- A strong focus—you must state your central idea clearly and completely
- Clear order—your ideas should be in an order that makes sense
- Good details—your ideas must have strong support

The person who scores your essay will use a **rubric.** A rubric is like a checklist. It goes over important points that should be included in an essay. You can use a rubric to judge and improve your own essay.

Trying It Out

Here are rubrics for two different kinds of essays. Use one of the rubrics to evaluate your essay from Lesson 5. If you answered Prompt A, use Rubric A. If you answered Prompt B, use Rubric B. Rate your writing from 1 to 5. The highest score is 5. The lowest score is 1.

Rubric (Prompt A)	Rubric for Informative Writing	Score (1–5)
Opening thought	The focus is clear.	
	The writing catches the reader's attention	
Body paragraph	The paragraph topics are clearly stated.	
	The writer's ideas are in an order that makes sense.	
	The writer uses details to support his or her ideas.	
Closing thought	The focus is stated again.	
	The body ideas are stated again.	
	The essay has a clear end.	
Entire essay	Grammar, spelling, and punctuation are correct.	

Rubric (Prompt B)	Rubric for Narrative Writing	Score (1–5)
Opening thought	The focus is clear.	
	The writing catches the reader's attention	
Body paragraph	The ideas are in an order that makes sense.	
	The writer uses details to create life-like pictures of people, places, and actions.	
	The setting is described clearly.	
	People seem real.	
Closing thought	The meaning of the story is clear.	
	The story has a clear end.	
Entire essay	Grammar, spelling, and punctuation are correct.	

Looking It Over

After you evaluate your essay, answer the questions below.

1. What are the best parts of your essay?

_____

_____

_____

_____

_____

2. What are your essay's weakest parts? How can you make them better?

_____

_____

_____

3. Choose the weakest part of your essay. Rewrite it to make it better.

_____

_____

_____

_____

CHAPTER 2 REVIEW

In this chapter you learned how to plan an essay. You have practiced writing focused, supported essays. You have also learned to judge how good your essay is.

Looking Back

Answer the questions below in the space provided.

1. What are three things you should try to find in a writing prompt?

_____

_____

2. What are two ways of prewriting to get ideas?

_____

_____

3. How do you decide what your focus will be?

_____

_____

4. Name two ways to order an essay.

_____

_____

5. What are three things you should look for after you write your essay?

_____

_____

Trying It Out

Answer the prompt below. Write your essay on your own paper.

Prompt Write about a time when a family member, friend, or someone else you know was proud of you.

DIFFERENT TYPES OF ESSAYS

Introduction

You have learned new skills to help you with your writing. Now, you can learn about the different types of writing. There are four basic types of essays. You use different kinds of essays to answer different kinds of questions. There are also different ways to plan each type of essay.

Informative Essay

An informative essay gives your reader information. In it, you use ideas or points to back up your main idea. An essay about why dogs act the way they do would be an informative essay. You can use this type of essay to write reports and business letters. A list is a good way to plan this essay.

Persuasive Essay

A persuasive essay tells readers what you believe. Its goal is to make readers agree with you. An essay that gives reasons why students should join a club would be a persuasive essay. Some prompts may ask you to write a speech or a letter instead of an essay. Use a list to plan this essay. Write down reasons that are likely to make readers agree with you.

Narrative Essay

A narrative essay tells a story. The prompt for this essay may be a picture. If you write a story about something you did, you are writing a narrative essay. A story web is a good tool for planning a narrative essay.

Descriptive Essay

A descriptive essay helps your reader see and feel a thing that you describe. The prompt for this essay may be a picture. An essay telling what your classroom looks like would be a descriptive essay. Use a numbered list to plan the essay. The list will help you to put your ideas in the best order.

Notice the things included in each kind of essay. Then, practice writing each type. In every essay, tell the reader what your focus is. Use plenty of details to back up the focus. This will make your essay easy to read.

Description of Different Types of Essays

Informative Essay: You write this type of essay to explain something. You can tell how things are different or alike. You can also give results or facts.

An informative essay should have the following:

- An **opening thought** with a clear focus sentence. You should give your main points. This lets your reader know what you will write.

- A **body** with a paragraph for each main point. Explain each point with details. Use good, solid facts to prove what you write.

- A **closing thought** that tells your focus again. Say it in a new way. Make it clear that you are ending your essay. Be careful not to put any new ideas here.

Informative Prompt Who is the most interesting person you know? Write an essay that tells what makes that person interesting.

Persuasive Essay: You write this type of essay to prove a point. The prompt will tell you about a subject that people disagree about. You must take a side. Then, you must tell how you feel and defend what you believe.

A persuasive essay should have the following:

- An **opening thought** that explains the argument. Choose a side. Write a focus sentence that makes your feelings clear.

- A **body** made of two or more paragraphs. In the body paragraphs, give the reasons for your feelings.

- A **closing thought** that tells your belief again. Remind your reader about your reasons. This helps the reader to remember your strong points. Do not put any new ideas in the closing thought.

Persuasive Prompt Some people want students to stop having recess. How do you feel about this? In a letter, convince your principal to agree with you.

Narrative Essay: This type of essay tells a story. When you write a narrative essay, you can make the story up, or use people and events from real life.

A narrative essay should have the following:

- An **opening thought** that lets your reader know about the setting and characters. Tell the reader anything needed to understand the story. Put your story's focus here.

- A **body** with one or more paragraphs that tell the story in order. The characters might talk in this kind of essay.

- A **closing thought** with a clear ending. Do not leave your reader wondering what happened. You can give your story a moral in the closing thought.

Narrative Prompt Sometimes, people spend a lot of time worrying about something. Later, they find out everything was okay. Write a story about a time when you worried over nothing. Tell what you learned from this event.

Descriptive Essay: You write this type of essay to tell about a thing, person, or event.

A descriptive essay should have the following:

- An **opening thought** that explains your focus. This paragraph should tell the reader what the topic is.

- A **body** of one or more paragraphs. Describe your topic in a way that makes it easy for your reader to understand. You may describe it from top to bottom or front to back. Describe your topic by using the five senses.

- A **closing thought** that tells your focus again. It should also tell how you feel about your topic.

Descriptive Prompt Imagine that you are caught outside in a storm. Write an essay that describes the storm.

Looking It Over

You read an essay that gives reasons why you should work hard in school. Which type of essay did you read?

Writing an Informative Essay

In school, you may need to write a report. You also may write to tell how two stories are different or alike. These types of writing are informative essays. Good writers **hook** their readers at the beginning. A hook gets the reader's attention. Some good hooks are surprising facts or jokes. Questions also work well.

These words let you know that the prompt is for an informative essay: **respond to, discuss, compare, contrast, define,** or **explain.**

Getting Started

Read the following prompt. See how the writer plans his essay. Then, read the essay.

> **Prompt** Many of us have role models in our lives. These are people we look up to. They can be family members, teachers, or coaches, for example. Who is your role model? Explain why you chose that person.

The writer used a list to plan his essay. It looked like this:

Coach Davis

- few good role models
- soccer coach—good role model for kids
- good player, good coach, went to college, works in town
- is nice to players, no put-downs
- helps players with their problems, listens

Coach Davis
by Marshall Jerowski

We are always hearing about sports players getting in trouble.   1
Children are left without good role models. Randy Davis's players,   2
however, have the best role model. Coach Davis is a good role model   3
for several reasons.   4

Coach Davis played soccer when he was young. He played forward   5
in high school and college. After college, he moved back home to   6
work. He soon realized that he missed soccer. He decided to become   7
a coach. He seems to know everything about the game. He knows   8
how to teach it to his players. Most of his players have never played   9
soccer before. Coach Davis starts slowly with the basic skills. The   10
players who listen and practice always get better.   11

One reason his players do well is that he treats them with respect.   12
Not all players are good athletes. Coach Davis works hard to teach   13
each one. He helps his players to try hard and do their best. He says   14
he wants every player to learn to enjoy soccer. He says that no one   15
can enjoy soccer if the coach is mean. Put-downs are against the   16
rules on the field. He does not call anyone names. He never says his   17
players are not playing well. He says that a group cannot be a team if   18
the players put each other down.   19

Coach Davis is a role model because he listens. If a player asks for   20
help with soccer, he gives that player extra attention. If a player has a   21
problem, he listens. He does not always have a way to solve every   22
problem. Still, he listens and tries to help if he can.   23

Sports stars today get into trouble a lot. Thank goodness kids have a   24
role model like Coach Davis. He is a good athlete, a great coach, and   24
a kind person. Players and parents love him. We all hope that he   26
keeps coaching for many years.   27

Looking It Over

Answer the following questions in the space provided.

1. How does Marshall try to get your attention in his opening thought?

   _____

   _____

2. Find Marshall's focus. Where is it? Is it clear to you?

   _____

   _____

3. Does Marshall mention his main points in his opening thought? Why or why not?

   _____

   _____

4. How does Marshall back up all of his main points in the body?

   _____

   _____

Trying It Out

It is time for you to write an informative essay. Read the prompt, and choose a focus. Organize your thoughts with a list. Choose points that you can explain well. Remember to back up each point that you make. Use your own paper.

Prompt Almost no one would turn down a million dollars, but what about a million of something else? If you could have a million of anything except dollars or money, what would it be? Explain your answer. Tell why you chose what you did.

Writing a Persuasive Essay

When you talk your brother into doing your chores, you are being persuasive. When you write a letter to say that students should have more food choices at lunch, you are writing a persuasive essay. In an essay, you should have good reasons to back up your ideas. Your strongest reason should go at the end of the body of your essay. That way, the reader will remember the best reason in the essay.

These words let you know that the prompt is for a persuasive essay: **agree/disagree, viewpoint, argue/argument, should/should not, issue, persuade, position,** or **support.**

Getting Started

Read the following prompt. See how the writer plans her essay. Then, read the essay. Be ready to answer the questions that follow.

Prompt Some people feel that tall advertising signs along the road make your town ugly. They want to make a law against building new signs. How do you feel about this idea? Write a letter to your town's mayor. In it, explain your beliefs about this plan.

The writer used a list to plan her essay. It looked like this:

<u>reasons we should not have tall advertising signs</u>

- the town would look nicer
- people could enjoy our town
- people should watch the road and not the signs
- people will buy something because they need it, not because a sign made them want it

Sample Essay

Dear Mayor Sullivan,

You are thinking about passing a law to keep tall advertising signs off   1
the roadsides. Thank you for noticing that our town looks worse each   2
time a sign is raised. The new law will help the town look better and   3
become safer. It will keep the town from being ugly. Also, it will keep   4
drivers' and shoppers' attention where it should be.   5

If we build fewer signs, our town will look much nicer. People will be   6
able to see our pretty buildings instead of a bunch of signs. Most of   7
us have old oaks in our yards, and they have the best branches for   8
climbing. People will enjoy the tall trees without having to look at   9
ugly ads hanging in the air. That would be good for everyone.   10

Drivers should watch the road and not the signs. Signs catch   11
people's attention. Imagine how many accidents would never   12
happen if signs were not there to bother drivers. It takes only a   13
couple of seconds to get in an accident. What if one driver looked   14
around at a sign and crashed?   15

These signs also make people buy things that they do not really   16
need. People should go shopping because they need something, not   17
because a sign makes them want something. If we got rid of some of   18
these signs, people might not waste their money.   19

I hope that you will pass this new law that will make our town   20
prettier and safer. These ugly signs do not do anything good for our   21
town. More people might want to live here if we did not have so   22
many ugly signs. We will be better off appreciating what we have in   23
our town instead of being told to buy things we do not need.   24

Yours truly,   25

Letitia Johnson   26

Letitia Johnson   27

Looking It Over

Answer the questions below in the space provided.

1. Look at Letitia's first paragraph again. Which side did she choose?

   _____

   _____

2. Which sentence does not belong in Letitia's essay?

   _____

   _____

3. Where does Letitia put her most important points?

   _____

   _____

4. Look at Letitia's last paragraph. How does Letitia state her focus again?

   _____

   _____

5. How does Letitia state her main reasons again in her last paragraph?

   _____

   _____

Trying It Out

It is time for you to write a persuasive essay. Tell your reader about your topic at the beginning. Take your best idea, and support it with good reasons. Put your reasons in an order that makes sense. Remember to end the body of your essay with your strongest reason. Use your own paper.

(**Prompt**) Imagine that you could have a new class in your school. It could be about anything you want as long as you were learning something new. What class would you want? Write an essay to convince other students that they should take this class.

Writing a Narrative Essay

When you tell your friend about a field trip you took, you are telling a narrative. When you write a story to tell your little sister or brother, you are writing a narrative essay. A narrative essay is a story. It should be written like a story. It should contain plot, description, and maybe even talking between characters. Good narrative writers hint at their main idea in the first paragraph. This helps the reader understand what the story will be about.

Certain words let you know that a prompt asks for a narrative essay. They are as follows: **remember, recall, story, tell, event,** and **experience.**

Hint for narrative essays: Do not use any word or phrase too many times. You do not want to write "suddenly" or "and then" over and over. If you do, the essay can become boring to the reader.

Getting Started

Read the following prompt. Look at how the writer orders his thoughts. Then, read the essay.

Prompt The weather can have a big effect on your day. Write an essay telling about a time the weather changed your day.

The writer used a story web to plan his essay. It looked like this:

Characters:
me and my mom, cousins
Aurelio and Elena

Setting:
morning at my house
during storm

**Never Complain
About Rain**

Events:
I am supposed to go camping
with my cousins, but the trip
gets rained out. We "camp" in
the living room.

Outcome:
I learn that you can use
your imagination; turn a
bad time into a good one

Never Complain About Rain
by Ruben Perez

When I woke up, it was raining. My mom's voice was ringing in my   1
ears. I just wanted to stay in bed. It was Saturday, but I had to get up   2
early to go camping with my cousins. I had never been camping   3
before. I thought it might be fun, but since it was raining we might   4
not even get to go.   5

"Get up, Ruben! Just in case," my mom called from downstairs.   6

"Here is your breakfast," Mom said when I went into the kitchen. She   7
placed a bowl of cereal and a glass of juice in front of me. I did not   8
touch them for a long time.   9

"What's wrong, Ruben?" she asked. "Do you feel sick?"   10

"No," I said. "I just hope we get to go."   11

"Don't worry," Mom said. "I know you're excited. We can all go   12
another time if this trip doesn't work out."   13

"Okay," I sighed, waiting for the rain to stop.   14

My cousins came over anyway. They had all their camping gear   15
packed. They brought their stuff into the living room, and we all sat   16
on the couch pouting.   17

"What a bunch of sad faces," my mom said. "Come on. Let's set up   18
camp and have some fun."   19

"What?" we all said. My cousins Aurelio and Elena looked at me.   20
They looked surprised. I shrugged my shoulders. I did not know what   21
my mom was up to, but she was unpacking our tent.   22

"Are we going to camp right here?" Elena asked.   23

"You bet," my mom said. Then, we all joined in to put up the tent.   24
We put our sleeping bags inside it and our flashlights outside it. "No   25
electricity tonight!" Mom said.   26

We even built a fire in the fireplace to roast hot dogs and   27
marshmallows. We used our flashlights when it got dark and slept in   28
the tent that night. We even told stories. The sound of the rain on   29
the roof made it seem as though we were out in nature somehow. It   30
even helped us sleep through the night.   31

I have been camping for real since then, but I still remember   32
camping in the living room. If it had not rained that day, I would   33
never have had that fun night with my mom and my cousins. On   34
that rainy night, I learned how we could turn a bad time into a good   35
time. We just had to use our imaginations!   36

Looking It Over

Answer the questions below on your own paper.

1. Read Ruben's first paragraph. What is the focus of his essay?

2. Who are Ruben's characters? What is the setting?

3. What background information does Ruben give early in the essay?

4. How does Ruben order events in the essay?

5. Look at Ruben's ending. How does he let you know the story is over?

Trying It Out

Use this prompt and picture to write a narrative essay. You will need to use your own paper.

Digital Imagery ©2000 PhotoDisc, Inc.

Prompt Write a story about the people in the picture above. Be sure to have a clear focus and clear order.

Writing a Descriptive Essay

When you tell what a person looks like, you are being descriptive. When you write a note to your friend to tell about a picture you drew for art class, you are writing a descriptive essay. Good writers use their senses to think of details for this type of essay. These kinds of details help the reader see, hear, smell, feel, or taste whatever is being described.

A prompt is probably asking for a descriptive essay if you see any of these words: **show, picture, senses,** or **describe/description.**

Getting Started

Read the following prompt. See how the writer orders her ideas. Then, read the essay. Be ready to answer the questions that follow.

Prompt Different seasons have different sights, sounds, and smells. Write an essay describing a season you enjoy. Set your essay in just one place. This might be your home, a park, or some other place you like to go.

The writer wrote about her home during the fall season. She made a chart to order her ideas. Her chart was based on the five senses.

sight	smell	sound	feel	taste
colorful leaves—red, yellow, and orange skies are blue or cloudy	leaves again pumpkin and apple pie smells apple cider	walking through leaves—kind of crisp and crackly	cool get to wear soft sweaters breezes blankets	different kinds of food pies and cider

A Fall Day
by Margot Goode

Fall is one of my favorite times. I like the way the air changes and
everything gets colorful. I like all the smells in the air. I like the way it
cools down, and I get to wear sweaters. I even like going back to
school. Spending a fall day at home to enjoy all the pretty changes is
something I really like.

Fall makes everything really beautiful. All the leaves change color.
The trees become red, orange, and gold. The sky is still blue most of
the time, and the leaves look very pretty against it. Even when the
sky is gray, the leaves keep our yard colorful. They fall all over the
ground, and the lawn barely shows through.

Fall feels good, too. I get to run around in sweaters and long-sleeved
shirts. They are soft and nice. I like it when the weather gets cool.
Outside, there are always breezes. My mom says it feels crisp. I think
this is a good word for it. I also like the feeling of being warm inside
the house when I know it is cool outside. I like crawling under the
blankets at night and feeling cozy.

The fall smell is really nice too. The leaves have a good smell when
you are outside. When you are inside, the house has nice fall smells
too. My dad likes to make pies. He makes apple pies and pumpkin
pies a lot in the fall. My mom likes hot apple cider. She makes it on
the stove with cinnamon. That is a really good smell.

All of these things make me like fall. I think it is the best season for
the senses. The weather changes from warm to cold, but you are
never too warm or too cold. You get to see all the pretty colors. You
get to smell all the good smells. I still like the other seasons. I would
not want fall to last all year long, but I am very glad I get to enjoy it
every year.

1
2
3
4
5

6
7
8
9
10

11
12
13
14
15
16

17
18
19
20
21

22
23
24
25
26
27

Looking It Over

Answer the questions below in the space provided.

1. Read Margot's first paragraph again. What is her focus? Is it clear?

   _____

   _____

2. Which of the five senses does Margot use in her essay?

   _____

   _____

3. Imagine that Margot wanted to write another paragraph. What might it be about?

   _____

   _____

4. Does Margot's conclusion remind you of her focus? If so, how?

   _____

   _____

Trying It Out

Read the following prompt. Write a descriptive essay. Tell your reader about your focus and topic early in the essay. Put your paragraphs in an order that makes sense. Describe every part of your topic. Use some of the five senses when you describe. Write your focus again at the end of your essay. Be sure to change the words you use. At the end of the essay, you should also tell your reader what you think about your topic. Use your own paper.

Prompt Most of us had a favorite toy when we were younger. What was your favorite toy? Write an essay that describes your favorite toy and tells what made it special.

CHAPTER 3 REVIEW

You have practiced writing four kinds of essays. You write each one for a different reason. Each essay has its own order. The informative gives information. The persuasive argues for your opinion. The narrative tells a story. The descriptive describes something using information from your senses.

Looking Back

Answer these questions in the space provided.

1. Name a good way to order each of the four essay types.

   _____

   _____

2. Think about the beginning of an informative essay. How can a writer catch the reader's attention? List two ways.

   _____

   _____

3. Which type of prompt may ask for a letter or speech instead of an essay?

   _____

4. List three words that let you know a prompt is for an informative essay.

   _____

5. What kinds of details should you use in a descriptive essay?

   _____

Trying It Out

Read the following prompt. Decide which type of essay you should use to answer the prompt. Then, write the correct kind of essay. Use your own paper.

Prompt Think about a place you like to go. Think of a place you dislike. Write an essay that tells what is different about these two places.

WRITING STRATEGIES FOR PROBLEM AREAS

Introduction

When you take a writing test, you must show that you know the rules for writing. Always use correct punctuation and spelling. Pay attention to sentence structure and other basic writing rules.

Sentence Structure

It is very important to use complete sentences. Sometimes, your sentences may not say enough. Then, your reader may not understand what you are trying to say. Other times, your sentences might say too much. Sentence fragments and run-on sentences are the names of these two problems. Luckily, both problems are easy to find and fix.

Punctuation and Capitalization

Punctuation and capitalization mistakes can confuse your reader. Help your reader understand what you are trying to say. Take the time to learn writing rules. There are rules for commas, semicolons, quotation marks, apostrophes, and capital letters.

Combining Sentences

Always state ideas as plainly as possible. If you are using the same words or phrases over and over again, join two or more sentences to form one sentence.

Paragraphs and Transitions

Always begin a new paragraph when you start to write about a new idea. Begin a new paragraph when your story starts to tell about a new action. When you move from one idea to another, you should use **transition** words. Transition words like "however" will help make your writing smooth. Using paragraphs and transitions will also help you to order your writing.

Using Words Properly

Spelling mistakes and misused words pull your reader's attention away from your focus. They can even confuse your reader. Pay special attention to **homophones.** Homophones are words that sound the same but have different spellings and meanings.

Sentence Structure

When you write, you should make sure that your sentences are whole and clear. Run-on sentences have too much information. They do not have enough punctuation. Every sentence needs a subject. A subject tells who or what does the action. You should also check to see that each sentence has a verb (an action). When you leave out your subject or your verb, you make a sentence fragment.

Run-on Sentences

Sometimes, you might write two or more sentences together without punctuation between them. That is called a **run-on sentence.** Run-on sentences can be very confusing. Your readers do not know where one thought ends and another begins. They cannot understand the information.

Example Run-on Sentence:

Shania looked at her father she smiled.

Here are two ways to fix run-on sentences:

- **Form two or more separate sentences.**

  Shania looked at her father. She smiled.

- **Join the complete thoughts with a comma and a connecting word such as *and, but, or,* or *so.***

  Shania looked at her father, and she smiled.

Sentence Fragments

A **sentence fragment** is a group of words that is missing either a subject or a verb. It does not have a complete thought. The missing information in a sentence fragment can cause confusion.

Example Sentence Fragment:

A girl in my class.

This sentence is about a girl, but it does not tell what the girl is doing. It does not tell what the girl is like, either. It can be fixed by adding a verb or a verb phrase.

Example Complete Sentence:

A girl in my class asked a question.

As you can see, you often need to add words to make complete sentences. Sometimes you can even attach a fragment to a nearby sentence.

Example Sentence Fragment:

Javier laughs at my jokes. Spends time with me.

Example Complete Sentence:

Javier laughs at my jokes and spends time with me.

Getting Started

Read the paragraph below. Look for sentence fragments and run-ons. Then answer the questions.

Sample Paragraph

Ariana's classmates were bubbling with excitement. Mrs. Wu had promised they could take a field trip. **(1) To the meadow.** They would study the insects that lived in the tall grass and flowers. **(2) They could eat a picnic there Mrs. Wu had even said they might have a bug hunt.** The students studied their lessons. They wanted to recognize the insects they saw. They would show Mrs. Wu what they had learned.

Looking It Over

1. Look at the sentences that are in bold print. Tell whether each group of words is a fragment (F) or a run-on (RO).

    (1) _____   (2) _____

2. Connect the word group **"To the meadow"** with a sentence near it. Make sure your new sentence makes sense. Write the sentence below.

    _____

    _____

3. Make the run-on sentence two separate sentences by using a period. Write the sentences below.

    _____

    _____

4. How do the mistakes make this paragraph harder to understand?

    _____

    _____

Trying It Out

Fix the fragments below. Mark corrections on the sentences.

1. Ran to the finish line.

2. After I left school.

3. Mr. Leota asked her to stop talking. Finish her practice sheet.

Fix the run-on sentences below. Make your marks on the sentences.

4. The striped cat ran out the door I tried to catch it.

5. I showed Albert my drawing he liked it.

6. In science we are learning about frogs they start out as tadpoles.

Capitalization and End Punctuation

Remember that small mistakes add up on writing tests. Be sure to use correct capitalization when you are writing. You should also be sure to place periods, question marks, or exclamation points after your sentences.

Capitalization

There are many capitalization rules. The rules listed below are the ones you will need most often. If you take the time to learn these, you can improve your test scores.

Things That Are ALWAYS Capitalized

- All proper nouns (the names of particular people, places, or things)

  Monday, Labor Day, World Series, Dodd Elementary School, Lake Travis, Library of Congress, Arkansas, José Morales

Things That Are SOMETIMES Capitalized

- A person's title **only** when it is used as a name or right before a person's name

  What do you think of our plan, **Mayor?** (used as a name)

  The **mayor** was unhappy with our plan.

  I told **Mayor Sigala** about the new plan. (used right before a name)

- Family words (such as *mom, dad, uncle,* and *aunt*) **only** when they are used as a name or right before a person's name

  I asked **Aunt** Yvonne for her cookie recipe. (used right before a name)

  I asked my **aunt** for her cookie recipe.

  Where is **Dad?** (used in place of a name)

  My **dad** works for the city.

- Directions **only** when they are names for areas

  Maria asked me to drive **south** toward the school.

  We once visited the **South.**

- Names of school subjects, unless they are language courses (**French, math**)

  I'll be studying **English history** this **spring.**

Things That Are NEVER Capitalized

- Names of seasons (**summer, fall, spring, winter**)

End Punctuation

When you write a sentence, you must end it with the correct punctuation mark. Most sentences end with a period, but not all of them do.

Always end a sentence that states something with a period.

> The frog hopped over my foot.

> I asked the police officer for directions.

Always end a question with a question mark.

> Is Quinn coming over to study later?

> When will Uncle Jay be finished with the computer?

Always end a strong feeling with an exclamation point.

> What a cold day this is!

End a command or a request with either a period or an exclamation point. Which one you choose depends on how forceful you want to be.

> Look out for that big hole!

> Come here, please.

Getting Started

Circle the mistakes in the following sentences. All of the mistakes are capitalization errors. Some sentences have more than one error.

1. My mom told me to turn south onto Ryan drive.

2. The Sloan Museum of Art is closed on mondays.

3. When did you call your Mother to ask about the birthday party?

Place the correct end punctuation on the next three sentences.

4. Watch out for the bee

5. When are you leaving for the baseball game

6. I wondered why the cat hid under the stairs

Looking It Over

Read the following prompt and paragraph. Look for mistakes in capitalization and end punctuation. Then, answer the questions.

(**Prompt**) Have you ever raised money for a cause? Write an essay that describes a good way people can earn money for a good cause.

Did you ever earn money for a cause. My Friends and I decided to earn money to donate to the Bankstown wildlife Rescue Center. We wanted to hold a car wash. Our parents helped us gather the supplies we needed. We asked a grocery store manager if we could use the parking lot for our car wash? We chose a day in late Spring to hold the wash. We had a lot of fun. We also earned money to donate. We were very proud of what we had done.

1. Circle the sentence that needs a question mark. Rewrite it correctly.

   _____

   _____

2. Circle the three capitalization errors. Rewrite the words correctly.

   _____

3. Circle a sentence that needs a period instead of a question mark. Rewrite it correctly.

   _____

   _____

Punctuation

Punctuation marks are like road signs for your readers. They help show which ideas belong together. If you do not punctuate well, you might confuse your reader. The reader could even miss the point you are trying to make.

Commas

One reason to use commas is to tell a reader when to pause. Commas can also keep readers from being confused. They do this by separating words that do not belong together. Some specific comma rules are stated below.

- Use commas to separate three or more items in a series.

  Cedric bought **apples, oranges, and bananas.**

  Tonight I **called Tom, baked a cake, and drew a picture.**

- Use a comma before a short connecting word (*and, but,* or *or*) if it is joining two complete thoughts.

  The kitten curled up on my lap. It slept peacefully.

  The kitten curled up on my lap, **and** it slept peacefully.

- Use commas around words that interrupt a sentence. Also, place commas after words that introduce a sentence. Put commas around words that are not necessary to the sentence.

  Our standards, **after all,** are very high.

  Mr. Villa, may I be excused?

  My friend, **who plays soccer,** likes to wear cleats.

Quotation Marks

- The exact words that someone said or wrote should be in quotation marks.

  (Notice how commas are used with quotation marks.)

  "The keys are on the table," said my brother.

- **Do NOT** use quotation marks when you tell about something a person said, thought, or wrote.

  My brother said that he would not go to practice tonight.

- Use quotation marks around nicknames or slang terms.

  In the 1960s, people called things **"groovy."**

  Our best hitter is Sam **"The Slam"** Duncan.

Apostrophes

- Use an apostrophe (') to show that someone owns something.
- If a noun is singular (only one), add **'s.**

  my sister**'s** cat, Leonardo**'s** mitt, Mr. Jones**'s** house

- If a noun is plural (more than one) and ends with **–s**, add only an apostrophe.

  my neighbor**s'** dog, the rabbit**s'** tails, the Fajardo**s'** car

- If a noun is plural but does not end in **–s**, add **'s.**

  the children**'s** coats, the mice**'s** cheese

- Use an apostrophe in contractions. Contractions have apostrophes where letters or numbers have been left out.

  do not—don't

  it is—it's

  1980—'80

Getting Started

Correct the punctuation errors in the following sentences. If there are no punctuation errors, write "correct" below the sentence.

1. The three kids coats were mixed up in the closet.

2. Lane asked me "if I would wash the car today."

3. Mr. Allen could I please be excused?

4. The cat walked across my path, but it did not see me.

5. My mother was born in the 60s.

6. Miguel asked, Do you want help with your history project?

Trying It Out

Read the following paragraph. Place the missing commas, quotation marks, and apostrophes in the paragraph. Do not add or take out words. Just add needed punctuation.

One night last summer I decided I wanted to camp. I pitched the tent and slept by myself in our backyard. You cant put up the tent by yourself said my mother but I did just fine. I was not afraid. I knew that my sister Janies dog would bark if anyone came into our yard. I brought a flashlight a sleeping bag a pillow and some snacks out with me. When I came into the house the next morning, my dad told me he was really proud of me. I said to him, I would like to camp for real sometime. He said he would go camping with me anytime I wanted.

Combining Sentences

Good writers use few words to make their points. When you are taking a writing test, pay attention to the words you use. Are you using the same words over and over? This is a clue that you should combine some of your sentences. Then, your writing will be more clear. There are many ways to combine sentences.

Using Modifiers to Combine

You might repeat words when you describe something or someone. You should try to put all the **modifiers** that describe the same thing into one sentence. (Modifiers are words or groups of words that describe.)

> **The bug was** green. **The bug was** big. **It was** hopping across our floor.

> **The big green bug was hopping across our floor.**

Using Phrases to Combine

Many times, you can join phrases. Phrases are groups of words. Joining phrases will help keep your writing from sounding choppy.

> **I worked** hard all day. **I was working** in the yard. **I was** helping my father.

> **I worked hard in the yard all day, helping my father.**

> Neema sat at her desk. She studied hard.

> **Neema sat at her desk and studied hard.**

Using Clauses to Combine

Sometimes, writers change their short sentences into clauses. A clause has both a subject and a verb. If you notice that your sentences are short and choppy, you might join some of them.

> Aunt Christie gave me a diary. I began writing every night.

> **After Aunt Christie gave me a diary, I began writing every night.**

Here are some more words that can be used to combine clauses: **when, before, since, until, during, while, because, instead of, and, or,** and **but.**

Getting Started

Combine the following sentences. Use the hints to help you with the first five sentences.

1. I looked for your lost cat. I looked everywhere. (Hint: modifier)

   _____

2. I fell off my bike. I skinned my knee. (Hint: phrase)

   _____

3. Keith and Manny went swimming. They swam in the city pool. They went on a hot day. (Hint: phrases)

   _____

4. Abel practiced a long time. He was going to play in the talent show. (Hint: clauses)

   _____

5. Maria mowed the yard. The yard was big. The yard was hilly. (Hint: modifiers)

   _____

6. We sat in the dark theater for two hours. It seemed really bright outside.

   _____

7. The little girl played. She played in her yard. She played with her puppy.

   _____

8. The chair was uncomfortable. The chair was old. It was green.

   _____

9. The party was over. It was a party for Ratasha's birthday.

   _____

10. Lucky chased his ball. He brought it back to me. He brought it back quickly.

    _____

Looking It Over

Read the following prompt. Then, read the paragraph. The paragraph is taken from an answer to the prompt. Look for repeated words and sentences that should be joined. Then, answer the questions.

Prompt Tell about a time you and your family had an exciting day. What happened? Was the whole day exciting? Write an essay that describes your day.

Sample Paragraph

Last week, our family went somewhere. We went to a water park. This park had seven slides. My cousin rode on all of them. I rode on all of them. Our favorite slide was tall. Our favorite slide was curvy. We rode it ten times. Then we felt a little bit sick. We didn't feel sick for long. We played at the park all afternoon.

Trying It Out

Combine the following sentences from the paragraph. Then, read the paragraph again. Ask yourself how combining sentences makes the paragraph easier to read.

1. Last week, our family went somewhere. We went to a water park. This park had seven slides.

   _____

2. My cousin rode on all of them. I rode on all of them.

   _____

3. Our favorite slide was tall. Our favorite slide was curvy.

   _____

4. Then we felt a little bit sick. We didn't feel sick for long.

   _____

Writing Paragraphs

When you are taking a writing test, you should always group details that belong together in paragraphs. Think of paragraphs as groups of ideas that belong together. Paragraphs help you order your supporting details. Anything written without paragraphs is hard to read and understand.

Topic Sentence

Each body paragraph should begin with a topic sentence. This sentence tells your readers what the paragraph is about. It helps keep them from being confused. It helps readers know why the information is in the paragraph.

Supporting Details

The supporting details are the middle part of your paragraph. This part will usually be three to five sentences long. Supporting details should explain, describe, and give examples.

Concluding Sentence

Each paragraph should end with a concluding sentence. This sentence is a signal to your reader that your paragraph has ended. It also shows that you are ready to move on to your next point.

Getting Started

Read the following prompt and the sample essay on the next page. Pay attention to the body paragraphs as you read. Then, answer the questions.

Prompt People celebrate holidays in their own ways. Choose your favorite holiday, and tell how you and your family or friends celebrate it.

My Favorite Holiday
by Frankie Nueva

A | Most every family celebrates special holidays. My favorite holiday is | 1
the Fourth of July. I guess some families just watch fireworks or have | 2
a picnic. My family likes to celebrate the whole day long. | 3

B | We begin the day by choosing special outfits. Every year, we try to | 4
outdo each other. We dress in red, white, and blue clothes. Last year, | 5
I wore a red-and-white-striped shirt with blue shorts. I had a sparkly | 6
red top hat on my head. There were silver streamers hanging from | 7
my sleeves. My mom and dad joined in the fun by wearing matching | 8
clothes. Their clothes were, of course, red, white, and blue. My | 9
family loves dressing up for the holiday. | 10

C | Each year, we also celebrate by inviting all of our friends to a big | 11
cookout. They all bring side dishes to go with the delicious food my | 12
mom grills. The only rule is that all the food must be red, white, or | 13
blue. This makes for some interesting potato salad. Eating together is | 14
fun, and the kids run around and play games all afternoon. Our | 15
cookout is a great way to spend our favorite holiday with our friends. | 16

D | The best part of Independence Day is watching the fireworks. When | 17
the sun starts to set, we all set up lawn chairs and put down | 18
blankets. Then, we watch the sky. After a hot summer day, the | 19
evening feels nice and cool. From our backyard, we can see the city | 20
fireworks display. We watch the sky the whole time so we will not | 21
miss any of the beautiful sparkles of light. | 22

E | As you can see, my family loves to celebrate the Fourth of July. | 23
Maybe it is because we have always been taught to be proud of | 24
where we come from. It is probably also because we like to dress | 25
silly, eat a lot of food, and watch fireworks. Whatever it is, I look | 26
forward to that day each year. | 27

Looking It Over

Answer the questions below. Use the space provided.

1. What is the **topic sentence** of paragraph B?

   _____

2. Find a detail in paragraph B that shows that Frankie's family chooses special outfits for this holiday. Write it below.

   _____

(continued on next page)

3. What is the topic of paragraph C?

   _____

4. What is the **concluding sentence** of paragraph C?

   _____

5. Paragraph D states that the best part of the day is watching fireworks. What does Frankie like about the fireworks?

   _____

6. Paragraph D does not have a **concluding sentence.** Write a **concluding sentence** for this paragraph.

   _____

   _____

Trying It Out

List three details or examples that would support the following topic sentence:

Learning to swim is very important.

   1. _____

   2. _____

   3. _____

Now, write a paragraph about the **topic sentence.** Be sure to use your details and examples to prove your point. Do not forget to write a **concluding sentence.**

Learning to swim is very important.

_____

_____

_____

_____

_____

Making Transitions

When you are taking a writing test, use **transitions.** Transitions are used to show how words, sentences, and ideas belong together.

Here are some sentences that use transitions:

Breakfast is an important meal. It can be tasty, **too.**

Some older dogs like to chew on things, **just as** puppies do.

Now that you have time, you should do your homework.

Transitions can add meaning to your writing in many ways. Here are some examples:

Transitions that add to ideas	besides, and, also, too, again, first, next, finally, last, not only
Transitions that show how things are different	but, yet, however, still, on the other hand
Transitions that show similarities	similarly, likewise, in a like manner, just as
Transitions that show results	therefore, as a result, so
Transitions that show time	meanwhile, immediately, soon, now, when, before, after, suddenly, during, finally, next
Transitions that show place	here, there, beyond, nearby, next to, under, near
Transitions that summarize ideas or make them stand out	in other words, for example, for instance, in fact, as you can see, clearly

Getting Started

Read the following prompt. Then, read the two body paragraphs from the essay on the next page. Pay careful attention to the transitions as you read. Then, answer the questions.

Prompt Think of a simple task you can do. It could be something you can make or cook, or it could be a game you can play. Write an essay that describes how to do this task.

Cooking scrambled eggs is pretty easy. **You should get an adult to** 1
help you with the stove. First, heat some butter in a small pan. 2
Keep the heat on low. Next, crack open two eggs, and pour them 3
into a bowl. Make sure you do not get any pieces of shell in the 4
bowl. Then add some milk and a little bit of salt and pepper. 5

Use a fork to break the yolks and stir everything together. Then, pour 6
the mix into a pan. Stir the eggs as they cook. When the eggs are 7
firm, remove the pan from the hot burner. Do not forget to turn off 8
the burner! **You are almost ready to eat.** 9

Looking It Over

1. List two transitional words or word groups that were used in lines 1–5.

   _____

2. Look at the bold sentence in lines 1–2. What are two transitions you
   could use in this sentence? (Hint: Show how things are different.)

   _____

3. List two transitional words or phrases that were used in lines 6–9.

   _____

4. Look at the bold sentence in line 9. What transition could you use at the
   beginning of this sentence?

   _____

5. How do transitions help readers?

   _____

   _____

Trying It Out

1. In the following sentences, fill in the blank spaces with transitions. Be sure your transitions make sense.

   a. Feeding the dog is supposed to be a chore. _____ , I like taking care of him.

   b. _____ I tried it, I found out that I like spinach salad.

   c. Playing baseball can be hard, _____ I still enjoy it.

   d. Finish your homework. _____ ,we can go to the park.

2. In the space below, write a paragraph explaining how to plant a seed. Use at least **three** transitional words or word groups in your paragraph. **Circle** these transitions.

   _____

   _____

   _____

   _____

   _____

   _____

   _____

   _____

   _____

   _____

Commonly Misspelled Words

When you are taking a writing test, it is important to spell words correctly. Misspelled words can draw your reader's attention away from your point. The message of your essay can be lost if there are too many misspellings.

Study this list. The words are spelled correctly in this list.

Commonly Misspelled Words

across	February	once
beautiful	finally	pleasant
business	forty	realize
character	government	since
clothes	immediately	speech
decision	interesting	surprise
different	knowledge	together
disappear	library	true
disappoint	minute	usually
doctor	necessary	Wednesday
experience	ninety	which

Getting Started

Read the following prompt and the sample essay on the next page. Look for misspelled words. All misspelled words in the sample essay come from the list. Answer the questions when you have finished.

> **Prompt** What is your favorite place to visit? Write a narrative describing a visit to your favorite place.

A Trip to the Beach
by Marisa Modano

My favorite place in the whole world is the beach. I love playing in   1
the waves and building sand castles. Each summer, my family piles   2
into our station wagon. We drive for many hours to reach the ocean.   3
Last summer's trip was the best beach trip ever.   4

My parents, my two brothers, and I all climbed into the car. We had   5
all of our beach things with us, too. We took buckets and pails,   6
towels, floats, picnic food and supplies, cloths to wear, and a big   7
beach umbrella. It was so early that the sky had barely turned pink,   8
but we didn't mind. We usully like to get there early. We like to find a   9
good spot. My brothers and I soon fell asleep as we drove out of   10
town toward the sea.   11

When we finely arrived, our whole family cheered. My parents settled   12
in under the umbrella. The rest of us ran tagether to the water. We   13
laughed and splashed each other for a while. Then, we built a sand   14
castle. We like to make castles with many towers. Wonce, we even   15
dug a knee-deep moat.   16

After playing in the surf, we sat down to a picnic lunch. I think the   17
view is beatiful there on the edge of the ocean. It is the best place to   18
eat that I know. We enjoyed good food and the nice wind in our hair.   19
I could smell the fresh salty air. I thought about how much I loved   20
the beach.   21

We were lucky enough to get to stay for a whole week. Since my   22
parents know how much we love the ocean, they did not make us   23
get into the car until the last minit. We rode home with salt water in   24
our hair and plesant memories in our minds.   25

Looking It Over

Answer the questions below in the space provided.

1. Circle two misspelled words in lines 5–11. Write the correct words below.

   _____

2. Circle three misspelled words in lines 12–16. Write the correct words below.

   _____

(continued on next page)

3. Circle all the misspelled words in lines 17–21. Write the correct words below.

_____

_____

4. Circle all the misspelled words in lines 22–25. Write the correct words below.

_____

_____

Trying It Out

Find and circle the misspelled words in the sentences below. Write the correct words on the lines provided. Sentences may have more than one misspelled word. They may have none at all. If there are no misspelled words, write "correct."

1. My mother took me to the docter on Wednesday.

_____

2. I must have counted ninty sheep before I got to sleep.

_____

3. Wich sandwich did you pick?

_____

4. Was the last test question tru or fals?

_____

5. You suprised me when you jumped out of that closet.

_____

6. The president is the leader of the United States goverment.

_____

7. I immediately knew that something was wrong.

_____

8. Did you hear the speach that my father gave last night?

_____

Commonly Misused Words

Homophones give some writers trouble. Homophones are words that sound the same, even though they are spelled differently and have different meanings. Learn these words, and use them correctly.

Common Homophones

- **ate**   Julie **ate** a taco.
  eight   I saw **eight** kittens.

- **blue**   Sam has a **blue** van.
  blew   The wind **blew**.

- **buy**   I want to **buy** a book.
  by   He walked **by** me.

- **fair**   Was the test **fair**?
  fare   I paid your cab **fare**.

- **flower**   Is this your **flower**?
  flour   **Flour** is used in bread.

- **for**   This gift is **for** Sarah.
  four   Alma drew **four** birds.

- **hear**   Can you **hear** me?
  here   Come **here,** please.

- **hour**   The class lasts an **hour**.
  our   Look at **our** carpet.

- **its**   The bird ate **its** seed.
  it's   **It's** really cold outside.

- **knot**   Can you tie a **knot**?
  not   I will **not** let you jump.

- **meat**   Beef is red **meat**.
  meet   I want to **meet** her.

- **new**   Look at our **new** fish.
  knew   I **knew** that boy.

- **one**   Bonnie has **one** cat.
  won   Jack **won** the contest.

- **red**   Adam wore a **red** tie.
  read   I **read** the instructions.

- **right**   I picked the **right** one.
  write   Do you **write** songs?

- **road**   I drove on a dirt **road**.
  rode   Khan **rode** the horse.

- **sea**   Sharks live in the **sea**.
  see   Can you **see** the door?

- **their**   They shut **their** eyes.
  there   Look over **there**.

- **threw**   Al **threw** a curve ball.
  through   Go **through** the door.

- **to**   I rolled it **to** you.
  too   You are **too** loud.
  too   She is loud, **too**.
  two   Grab **two** sheets.

- **weak**   I felt **weak**.
  week   It lasts for a **week**.

- **who's**   **Who's** the new kid?
  whose   **Whose** ball is that?

- **your**   Here is **your** cap.
  you're   **You're** a nice person.

Getting Started

Circle the words that belong in each of the following sentences.

1. After practicing for an (hour, our), our soccer team felt (weak, week).

2. We bought those (flowers, flours) (for, four) (hour, our) coach.

3. Some of my friends do not like (to, too) eat (meat, meet).

4. (Its, it's) (knot, not) (fair, fare) when one child gets special favors.

5. I (hear, here) that (its, it's) (knot, not) easy to untie a (knot, not).

Looking It Over

Read the following paragraphs. The homophones are in **boldface.** Correct the misused homophones. Mark your corrections on this page. Not all boldface words will be incorrect.

A. I could **knot** believe it. Rafael was running **threw** the hall to his room. He was late **too** class again. The teacher had told him, "**Your** going to be in trouble if **you're** late **won** more time." He **new** the teacher would be mad. He told her that he was sorry. Even so, she had him **right** her a note explaining why he was late.

B. Last winter, my family visited the mountains for a **weak.** None of us had ever been **there** before. We even needed to use a map to find the **right rode.** It was **not** as snowy **their** as I had thought it would be. Still, I almost turned **blew** with cold. I did see some beautiful sights. Also, I got to **meat** a new friend. The **to** of us were together most of the time.

C. "**Whose** your best friend?" I heard a voice ask. I **knew write** away who was asking. I would **no** that voice anywhere. I turned around to **see** my best friend, Jill, smiling at me. It wasn't even a **fare** question. She has been my best friend since kindergarten. We have been friends **threw** thick and thin. We're like **too** peas in a pod. I grinned back at Jill. We laughed as we walked to **hour** classroom.

Trying It Out

Write a paragraph that uses the following words correctly. Write about any topic. Circle the words where they appear in your paragraph. Use the space provided.

flower	see
one	their
red	knew
write	here

_____

_____

_____

_____

_____

_____

_____

_____

_____

_____

_____

_____

_____

Writing on Your Own

Read the prompt below. Then write an answer to the prompt. As you write, remember to use what you have learned in the lessons of this chapter.

Prompt Everyone's bedroom is different. Some people share a bedroom. Describe your bedroom, explaining how your bedroom or parts of your bedroom let people know what you are like.

Remember the steps in writing a good essay.

Step 1. Write down the topic, audience, and purpose of an essay that responds to the prompt.

_____

_____

_____

Step 2. Use one of the prewriting methods you learned in Chapter 2, Lesson 2, to find ideas for your essay.

Step 3. Look at your prewriting, and write a focus for your essay. Review Chapter 2, Lesson 3, if you need help.

_____

_____

Step 4. Use one of the methods you learned in Chapter 2, Lesson 4, to order your essay's paragraphs.

(continued on next page)

Step 5. Write your essay on the lines below. Keep in mind everything that you learned in this chapter.

_____

_____

_____

_____

_____

_____

_____

_____

_____

_____

_____

_____

_____

_____

_____

_____

_____

_____

_____

_____

_____

_____

_____

_____

_____

_____

Evaluating Your Writing

In this chapter, you have learned many useful rules for writing. When you take a writing test, you will need to use these rules. To see how well you have learned them, look at the essay you wrote on page 80 and answer the questions below.

1. List the transitions you used. You should have **at least two** transitions in each paragraph. If you do not, add more transitions.

    _____

    _____

    _____

    _____

2. Find three places in your essay where sentences need to be combined. Write your new sentences below.

    _____

    _____

    _____

    _____

3. Quietly, read your paper out loud. Check to make sure you have commas only where they are needed. Remove any commas that are not needed. If you used a comma incorrectly, write the corrected sentence or sentences below.

    _____

    _____

    _____

(continued on next page)

4. Circle any words that you think may be misspelled. First, look for the words on the list in Lesson 7. If you do not find them there, look them up in a dictionary. Correct any words that are misspelled. List the correct spellings below.

_____

_____

5. As you read over your essay, underline any homophones. Double-check these words. Be sure you have used the correct word. Make any changes needed. List the homophones and the changes you made below.

_____

_____

_____

_____

6. What is the best thing about your essay? Why do you think so?

_____

_____

_____

_____

_____

7. What is the main thing you could do to improve your writing? What are some ways you can improve in this area?

_____

_____

_____

_____

_____

CHAPTER 4 REVIEW

What you say on a writing test is very important. But how you say it is just as important. Always pay attention to spelling, capitalization, punctuation, and word choice.

Looking Back

Circle and fix the mistakes in the following sentences.

1. My Dad and I ate for sandwiches. After we finished swimming.

2. Mrs. Jimenez told me that "The door was already locked."

3. My familys trip to the libary was cut short the libary closed early.

4. If you drive South accross the River, you will find Westview street.

5. Why are you staring at me.

Combine and rewrite the following sentences. Use the space provided.

6. Sasha knocked on the door. She knocked lightly. She did not want to wake up the sleeping baby.

   _____

7. I put the books on the shelf. I put them in the classroom. The books were heavy.

   _____

8. I walked home today. I walked from school. I did not have a ride.

   _____

Trying It Out

Read the prompt below. Use your own paper to write your response to the prompt.

Prompt A new student is coming to your classroom. He needs to know your classroom rules and routines. Write him a letter telling him what to expect. Tell him what he needs to know about your class in order to do well at school.

REVISING YOUR ESSAY

Introduction

The last step in writing a good essay is revising. As you revise, try to put yourself in your reader's place. Look for mistakes. Then, fix as many mistakes as you have time to fix. Make sure you have answered the prompt. Check to make sure your writing has a focus. Check each paragraph and sentence to make sure each is complete and correct. You might even write a paragraph or two over again.

Looking for Mistakes

When you revise, the first step is to read your essay carefully. Look for mistakes as you read. Make sure your paragraphs are in the best order. Make sure each sentence is a complete thought. Also look for run-on sentences. Try to find misspelled words.

Deciding What to Fix

When you take a writing test, you have only a few minutes to revise. You may not have time to fix every mistake that you find in your essay. First, correct the errors that would keep readers from understanding your writing. Then, go back to smaller errors.

Checklist for Revisions

A checklist for revisions will help you do well on a writing test. Use a checklist for revisions when you revise. A checklist for revisions will remind you what to look for. Your checklist for revisions might ask questions like the following:

- Does your writing have a focus?

- Is each sentence a complete thought?

- Is each word spelled correctly?

Looking for Mistakes

Once your essay is written, you can begin revising. Read through your essay slowly and carefully. Look at each sentence. Make sure it is a complete thought. Check for misspelled words. Add any missing words. Be sure your essay has a focus.

Getting Started

Read the prompt and the essay. Notice the changes Jake has made. When you finish, answer the questions.

Prompt Write an essay about the job you want to have when you grow up. Give reasons for your answer.

Sample Essay

Mr. Anderson, the Teacher
by Jake Anderson

I ~~teached~~ <u>have taught</u> other people for as long as I can remember. I   1
have six younger brothers and sisters, <u>so</u> I know a lot about children.   2
One of my chores is to help my sister Carrie and my brother Marc.   3
~~W~~ <u>with</u> their homework. They say~~s~~ I am a good teacher because I am   4
very ~~patience~~ <u>patient</u>. When I grow up, I would like to be a teacher.   5

I want to be a teacher because being around kids is a lot of fun. I like   6
to make them happy. My favorite teachers are the ones who make   7
~~there~~ their classes ~~more funner~~ <u>fun</u>. When I am a teacher., I will make   8
sure my students have a good time in class. Who says learning can't   9
be fun?   10

I think teachers are some of the most important people in the world..   11
~~y~~You have to be smart to be a teacher. I know I will have to study   12
~~more~~ hard for a long time ~~to be a teacher~~. But I think all the hard   13
work will be worth it. <u>I would like to hear kids call me "Mr.</u>   14
<u>Anderson" some day.</u>   15

Looking It Over

1. Find Jake's focus sentence. Write that sentence here.

    _____

    _____

2. Look at lines 11–12. Why did Jake split these lines into two sentences?

    _____

    _____

3. Why did Jake add the last sentence in lines 14–15?

    _____

    _____

Trying It Out

Read the prompt and the essay. Look for mistakes in the essay. Correct these mistakes. You should add one new sentence to the essay.

Prompt Your city council is thinking about a curfew of 9:00 P.M. each night. Your teacher feels that a nine o'clock curfew will help students get a good night's rest. She thinks students will learn better if they are rested. Write an essay saying whether you agree with your teacher's thoughts. Explain the reason for your answer. Write an essay explaining why you agree or disagree with the new rule.

Sample Essay

Nine Is Too Early
by Joel Weiss

Making students be home 9:00 is not fair. Some students do not	1
need that much sleep. I goes home by at 9:30, I am hardly ever tired	2
in the morning. I am also a good student. I don't to go to bed that	3
early. My parent's let me stay out longer because I has a lot of	4
energy. What is right for one student, may not be right for another.	5
Being home by 9:00 will also make students unhappy. My family and	6
me go bowling at 9:00. If I had to go home. I would not be able to	7
do this. I would feel left out. No one wants to feel that way. That	8
does not help them do their better in school.	9

Deciding What to Fix

A writing test is usually timed. You may have only a few minutes to revise. And you may not have time to fix every mistake you find. For example, your essay could have both big and small mistakes. In that case, you do not want to spend all of your time fixing small mistakes. When revising, first make sure your essay has a focus. Make sure each of your paragraphs supports your focus. Then, fix any other errors you notice. Look for sentence fragments. Have you spelled any words incorrectly? Have you left out any words?

Getting Started

Read the prompt. Then, read the essay. Look at Yin's changes.

> **Prompt** Your teacher has asked you to write an essay. You are writing to a new student who is visiting your town. The student will visit for a few weeks in the summer. Tell the student what your town is like. Also, tell about a few of your favorite places.

Sample Essay

About Eastdale
by Yin Kwong

My name is Yin Kwong, and I've lived in Eastdale all of my ~~whole~~ life.   1
Eastdale is a nice town,. ~~n~~Not much happens here, but it is very   2
pretty. The people are friendly and kind. Two places you must <u>go</u>   3
while you are in Eastdale are Al's Pizza and Kirby Park.   4

Al's Pizza is on Third Street. Al owns the restaurant, he makes the   5
best pizza in the whole world. He'll make your pizza any way you like   6
it<u>.</u> He'll add extra cheese or mushrooms even if you only order one   7
slice. ~~Al used to live in Italy~~. Al also makes really good sandwic<u>h</u>es. His   8
egg salad sandwich is my favorite.   9

Kirby Park is the prettiest place in Eastdale. It has a big pond, with   10
lots of ducks and fish. The playground in the park is nice to<u>o</u>. You   11
can also go for walks. You can walk along a pretty trail. Eastdale can   12
be a nice place to visit. I hope you have a ~~nice~~ <u>good</u> time!   13

Looking It Over

1. Look over Yin's essay. What types of changes did she make?

   _____

   _____

2. If Yin had more time, what other changes could she have made? Circle a sentence that she could have revised. Write the revised sentence below.

   _____

   _____

Trying It Out

Read the prompt and sample essay below. Circle the four errors that you would change first. Make only **four** changes to the essay.

Prompt We remember certain times in our lives because they were special. Name a time in your life that was special. Write an essay telling your teacher about it.

Sample Essay

Our Weekend at the Beach
by Erin Kim

I will never forget one weekend with my brother Simon. We spent it	1
at our Aunt Sarah's house. By the beach. Me and Simon live in Ohio.	2
We don't get to go to the beach that much. My Aunt Sarah and	3
Uncle Phil live about a block from the beach.	4
The weekend was special because it was so beutiful. The weather was	5
great, the beach was filled with kids. Many of these kids were surfing,	6
swimming, and playing in the sand. It was wonderful to spend our	7
days in the sunshine and warm water. It was also nice to relax and	8
not worry about having to do nothing. At night we ate steamed	9
seafood and fly kites on the beach. Our weekend at the beach was	10
very special to me.	11

Checklist for Revisions

Use a checklist for revisions to help you revise. You might not have time to check everything on the list during a writing test. List the most important items first. That way, you may have time to check those.

Getting Started

Read each item on this checklist for revisions.

1. Does your essay answer the writing prompt?
2. Does your essay have a clear focus?
3. Does the body of your essay support your focus?
4. Does your essay have a closing thought?
5. Does each paragraph have a topic sentence?
6. Does each paragraph talk about only one idea?
7. Are there smooth changes between paragraphs?
8. Does your essay have a title?
9. Have you combined short sentences?
10. Have you crossed out any sentences that repeat what you have already said?
11. Is each sentence a complete thought?
12. Have you fixed all run-on sentences?
13. Have you checked to make sure you have not left out any words?
14. Have you crossed out any words you do not need?
15. Do your verbs match your subjects?
16. Does each pronoun match the noun it refers to?
17. Is each of your sentences punctuated properly?
18. Is each word spelled correctly?
19. Does the verb tense stay the same? If it changes, is there a good reason?

Looking It Over

1. Look over the checklist one more time. Make sure you understand everything on the list. Circle an idea you are unsure about. Then, write down what it means.

_____

_____

2. Write another item for the checklist. The item should help you with your own writing.

_____

_____

CHAPTER 5 REVIEW

In this chapter, you learned how to revise your writing. Revising can help you write a good essay. When you take a writing test, you may not have a lot of time to revise. You may be able to fix only a few mistakes. Always fix the most important mistakes first. Follow these steps to take when you revise an essay for a writing test:

● look for mistakes

● decide which mistakes to fix

● use a checklist to help you revise

Now that you have learned how to revise your writing, you are ready to do well on writing tests.

Trying It Out

Read the prompt below. Write an essay that responds to the prompt. Use your own paper. Use your checklist for revisions to revise your writing.

Prompt We all have things we would like to learn. Perhaps you would like to learn how to play a sport or a musical instrument. Choose a skill you would like to learn. Explain why you would like to learn this skill.

OTHER KINDS OF WRITING FOR TESTS

Introduction

Most writing tests will ask you to write an essay like the four you learned about in Chapter 3. Sometimes a writing test will ask you to write different things. You might be asked to write a letter or a report. Letters and reports are very much like essays. Focus, order, and support are still important. However, letters and reports have a different form and audience. An audience is a reader or group of readers.

Some prompts may ask for the following types of writing:

- **Friendly letter:** You write a letter to a friend or relative. You may also write to a person you have met, but do not know well.

- **Business letter:** You write a letter to a person in business. You may also write to a town or school leader, or to a newspaper or magazine editor.

- **Report:** You write a short report based on a list of facts. This kind of report contains information. For this reason, it will be a lot like an informative essay.

Remember that a letter has a specific audience. You have probably written a letter to a friend. In this case, your friend is your audience. You may be asked to write a letter like this on a test. This type of letter can be fun to write. However, it should never be sloppy.

You may need to write a business letter or report. Then, your letter should use more serious language. You may write a letter to the editor of a newspaper. This type of letter is written to be printed in the newspaper. In this case, the editor is not your audience. Your audience is the newspaper's readers.

On any writing test, your writing should show how well you can write. A letter to a friend will be judged the same way an essay will be judged. Your letter should have a strong focus with good support. It should be ordered well. It should show good grammar, punctuation, and sentence structure.

Letters and Reports

The parts of a **friendly letter** are

- date
- salutation (Dear _____ ,)
- body

- closing (Sincerely,)
- signature

A **business letter** has all of the parts of a friendly letter and adds

- heading (sender's address)
- inside address (receiver's)

- typed name and title under the signature

The business letter salutation ends with a colon instead of a comma.

Getting Started

Read the following prompt and letter. Then, answer the questions.

> **Prompt** Write a letter to a friend to encourage him or her to vote for a favorite teacher for "Teacher of the Year."

Sample Letter

April 15, 2001	1
Dear Ben,	2
What do you think about voting for Mrs. Sanchez for Teacher of the	3
Year? We will vote next week. I am going to vote for her. I know she	4
helped both of us with our reading. I bet you will want to vote for	5
her, too.	6
I think Mrs. Sanchez is a great teacher. Don't you? She is always in a	7
good mood. She tries very hard to help us learn. I love going to her	8
class, and I know you do, too.	9
I hope you will vote for her. I think she really deserves to win. Do not	10
forget to vote! The voting happens during lunch on Wednesday.	11
Yours truly,	12
Yuki	13

Looking It Over

1. Look at Yuki's letter. Now imagine that Yuki is going to send the letter to her principal. She would need to write it like a business letter. What parts would Yuki add? Tell how she would change the greeting.

_____

_____

_____

_____

Trying It Out

Answer the prompts below on your own paper.

Letter Prompt Imagine you have a new pen pal. Write a letter to your pen pal. Tell your pen pal about yourself and where you live. Ask your pen pal questions. Think about what you would like to know about him or her.

Report Prompt Your teacher wants you to write a report. The topic is redwood trees. Below are the notes you took. Write a short report using your notes.

Notes:

- Largest living things on earth
- Grow in Northern California; grow near the coast and other places
- Some grow over 300 feet high—taller than the Statue of Liberty!
- Usually about 8 feet to 20 feet wide
- Were here when dinosaurs walked the earth
- The kind near the coast in Northern California need fog and cool temperatures. They need these things to reach their full size
- The trees are very strong

GLOSSARY

body: the middle paragraphs of an essay. Pages 8, **14–15.**

brainstorming: a way of prewriting. When brainstorming, the writer puts down any idea that comes to mind. Usually the writer will write ideas in a list. Page **24.**

closing thought: the last paragraph of an essay. The closing thought talks about the essay's focus and main points again. It also brings the essay to a close. Pages 8, **14–15.**

descriptive essay: an essay that describes things, places, or people. Pages 38, 40, **50–52.**

focus: the main idea of an essay. The focus is sometimes called the central idea. Pages **8,** 10, 21, 27.

freewriting: a prewriting method. Writers freewrite to get ideas. They write down any idea that comes to mind. When writers freewrite, they usually write down phrases and sentences. Page **24.**

informative essay: an essay that tells the reader something new. The goal of an informative essay is to tell new information. Pages 38, 39, **41–43.**

letter to the editor: a persuasive letter. This kind of letter is written to the editor of a newspaper or magazine. However, it is written to be read by newspaper readers. Pages **91,** 93.

logical order: a way to order an essay by groups. These groups fall together because they make sense together. For instance, an essay about pets might talk about cats in one section. The next section might be about dogs. A third section might be about hamsters. Page **30.**

narrative essay: an essay that tells a story. Pages 38, 40, **47–49.**

opening thought: the first paragraph of an essay. The opening thought states the topic and tells the essay's focus. Pages 8, **14–15.**

GLOSSARY

order of importance: a way to put an essay in order. Some paragraph topics are more important than others. The essay is ordered by how important the topics are. Ideas are often ordered from least important to most important. Page **30.**

order of place: a method of ordering an essay. The essay is ordered by location. For example, imagine an essay that describes a mall. It would start at one end of the mall. It would tell about each store until it came to the other end of the mall. Page **30.**

persuasive essay: an essay that persuades the reader to believe something or to take some action. Pages 38, 39, **44–46.**

prompt: an essay question. A prompt is usually a short paragraph. It gives an essay topic. It also tells the audience for the essay. It tells the purpose of the essay. Some prompts include a picture. The picture is there to help the writer find ideas. Pages 21, **22–23.**

revision: working to improve an essay. Revision happens after a first draft is written. Pages 35–36, 81–82, **85–90.**

rubric: a checklist of the most important parts of a good essay. A rubric is used as a tool. It is used to grade or judge writing. Pages **18**–19, 35–36.

salutation: the greeting in a letter. It usually looks like this: "Dear _____ " It is then followed by a comma or a colon. Page **92.**

supporting details: ideas within a paragraph. These ideas support the topic sentence of the paragraph. There are usually several of them. They are found in each body paragraph. Page **67.**

time order: a way of ordering an essay. Events are written down in the order they happened. Page **30.**

topic sentence: a sentence that states the main idea of the paragraph. It is often at the beginning of a paragraph. Topic sentences are found in the body paragraphs of an essay. Page **67.**

Test-Taking Tips

In this book, you have learned many useful skills to help you succeed on writing tests. Here are a few additional test-taking hints.

- Be sure that you are well-rested and physically ready for the test. Get a good night's sleep. Be sure to eat a good breakfast. Avoid drinking anything with caffeine before the test. Caffeine can make you nervous and interfere with your ability to think. Visit the bathroom before the test begins.

- Wear comfortable clothes. Bring a sweater in case the room is cold.

- Bring pens, pencils, erasers, and anything else you will need.

- Before the test, take a moment to relax. Take a deep breath, and remind yourself that you are prepared. Tell yourself that you have been taught well and that you will do well on the test. If you feel tense, you can squeeze the desk with your hands to release tension. Breathing deeply and slowly will also help you relax.

- When the test is handed out, quickly scan the prompts to see how many essays you will need to write. Be sure to check the instructions so that you know whether you will need to respond to all of the prompts or just some of them.

- Read each prompt twice before writing.

- Take note of how much time you have to finish the test. Budget your time so that you have time to prewrite. Leave time for revising, but schedule most of your time for writing.

- Do not start writing until you have a plan for your essay. Complete your essay before you start revising. On most tests, it is more important to have a complete essay than a perfect one.